Seahorses

by Grace Hansen

ABDO
OCEAN LIFE
Kids

abdopublishing.com

Published by Abdo Kids, a division of ABDO, PO Box 398166, Minneapolis, Minnesota 55439.

Copyright © 2015 by Abdo Consulting Group, Inc. International copyrights reserved in all countries. No part of this book may be reproduced in any form without written permission from the publisher.

Printed in the United States of America, North Mankato, Minnesota.

102014

012015

 THIS BOOK CONTAINS RECYCLED MATERIALS

Photo Credits: Corbis, Glow Images, iStock, Minden Pictures, Shutterstock, Thinkstock

Production Contributors: Teddy Borth, Jennie Forsberg, Grace Hansen

Design Contributors: Laura Rask, Dorothy Toth

Library of Congress Control Number: 2014943721

Cataloging-in-Publication Data

Hansen, Grace.

Seahorses / Grace Hansen.

p. cm. -- (Ocean life)

ISBN 978-1-62970-711-2 (lib. bdg.)

Includes index.

1. Seahorses--Juvenile literature.   I. Title.

597/.6798--dc23

2014943721

Table of Contents

Seahorses 4

Food and Eating 14

Special Fish. 16

Baby Seahorses 20

More Facts 22

Glossary 23

Index 24

Abdo Kids Code. 24

Seahorses

Seahorses live in **shallow** tropical ocean waters.

5

Seahorses range in size.

They can be less than

one inch (2.5 cm) long.

They can be more than

14 inches (36 cm) long.

A small **dorsal fin** on its back helps it swim. Two **pectoral fins** on its sides help it steer.

pectoral fin

dorsal fin

9

A seahorse has a special tail. It uses its tail to hold onto plants.

11

Seahorses have very good eyesight. This keeps them safe from **predators**. It also helps them find food.

Food and Eating

Seahorses mostly eat

plankton. Their long

snouts suck in the food.

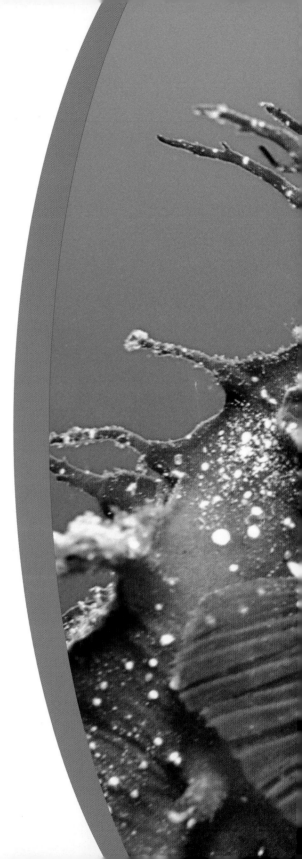

14

Special Fish

Males and females greet each other each morning. Most species stay together for life.

16

A male seahorse has a pouch. He carries eggs inside the pouch. This is very different from other animals.

Baby Seahorses

Males carry the eggs for a few weeks. Baby seahorses are on their own after they hatch.

More Facts

- Seahorses do not have teeth or a stomach. They eat almost constantly to stay alive.

- Seahorses are not good swimmers. They travel more easily by holding onto pieces of floating seaweed.

- A seahorse can change shape and color to blend in with its **environment**.

Glossary

dorsal fin – a fin used to move that is found on a seahorse's back.

environment – everything that surrounds and affects a living thing.

pectoral fins – a pair of fins just behind a seahorse's head used for steering.

plankton – very small animals that drift through the ocean.

predator – an animal that lives by eating other animals.

shallow – not deep.

Index

babies 20

eggs 18, 20

eyesight 12

fins 8

food 12, 14

habitat 4

predator 12

size 6

snout 14

tail 10

abdokids.com

Use this code to log on to abdokids.com and access crafts, games, videos, and more!

Abdo Kids Code:
OSK7112